SAT
BRONX

Do You Know
What Bronx Kids Know?

Students from Bronx Leadership Academy 2

Shannon O'Grady

Kristin Ferrales

Kathleen Cushman

All of the above

A project of Adobe Youth Voices

with What Kids Can Do, Inc.

NEXT GENERATION PRESS

Copyright © 2008 by What Kids Can Do, Inc.

A project of Adobe Youth Voices with What Kids Can Do, Inc.

Printed in Hong Kong by South Sea International Press Ltd.
Distributed by Next Generation Press, Providence, Rhode Island

ISBN 978-0-9815595-0-6
CIP data available.

Book design by Kathryn Van Syckle
Cover design by Sandra Delany
Cover photograph by Will Okun

Next Generation Press, a not-for-profit book publisher, brings
forward the voices and vision of adolescents on their own lives,
learning, and work. With a particular focus on youth without
economic privilege, Next Generation Press raises awareness
of young people as a powerful force for social justice.

Next Generation Press, P.O. Box 603252, Providence, RI 02906
www.nextgenerationpress.org

10 9 8 7 6 5 4 3 2 1

CONTENTS

Who Made This Test?

THIS BOOK RESULTS from a yearlong conversation among fourteen high school students, two teachers, and a journalist in the Bronx, New York. For three hours every week, we became co-authors, investigating issues that mattered to the lives and learning of urban youth, both in and out of school.

The students spoke about violence in the streets, at home, and in school. They talked about systemic inequities that affect their access to educational opportunity. They grappled with their views on military recruitment of minorities in a time of unpopular war. They probed what it means to be American yet to maintain allegiance to a minority ethnic heritage. They talked about what it takes to succeed in college. They created definitions for their specialized insider vocabulary.

Often, students spoke of the bias of the standardized tests that overshadow their schooling and decide their futures. In contrast, they described how they themselves assess intelligence, and what being "smart" requires of them. As much as the adults on our team questioned them, they questioned us. All of us began to realize how much they knew that we didn't know. One day, they created a multiple-choice test for the journalist, Kathleen Cushman, a middle-aged white woman who had just moved to New York. On a hard plastic chair-desk she sweated her way through it, as they watched with broad grins. Out of 50 items, she got one right—and that by guessing.

To make that very point, we chose to write this book in the form of a standardized test. As you read each section and answer its questions, we hope you will find out more of what you "know" and "don't know" about minority youth in urban schools.

SAT Bronx is not an easy test to take. Its passages contain "insider language" that you may not know if you are not part of an urban youth culture. The readings may rest on assumptions or prior knowledge that you might not share. To answer the test questions, you often must understand not only what the passages "mean" to you, but also how other people might think about them. Also, this test does not attempt to cover everything; instead, it dips into a few content areas and skill sets. It takes a snapshot of your knowledge, at a particular moment on a particular day.

However, in some ways, this book is more of a practice test than a real one. We do not require you to "bubble in" the answers on a separate sheet, and at the end of every section we put an answer key. You can take all the time you need. In fact, we want you to share your thoughts with others, and so we have included discussion prompts after each section for this purpose. As we all know, on tests like these, sometimes more than one answer can be right.

If you are an educator, we hope that digging into these Bronx students' perspectives will help you reflect on your own practice and hone your listening and comprehension skills. If you are a student, we hope that you will tell adults more about what you know, and gain confidence in your ability to excel in putting that knowledge onto the page in many different contexts. The last section of this book offers suggestions for use with both youth and adults.

Fairly or not, how people do on tests often determines their later success in life. We hope this one will do that in a good way, by helping people think again about what urban youth already know and can do.

Kathleen Cushman,
writer and editor, What Kids Can Do
Shannon O'Grady, teacher and writer
Kristin Ferrales, teacher and writer
and students from Bronx Leadership Academy 2

New York City, 2008

Words You'll Need For the Test

R EADING THE PASSAGES and questions in this test booklet, you may come across unfamiliar vocabulary. This section helps you prepare for that challenge, providing definitions for a sampling of colloquial terms used by the students who helped to write *SAT Bronx*.

Since word usage continually evolves and also varies considerably by region, you should treat this only as one local snapshot of informal speech, not an authoritative dictionary. Even youth from the same neighborhood and school often disagree on the meaning and proper usage of a word or phrase. However, reviewing these terms at the start may help you do better on the test ahead. Good luck!

1-D *(noun)* one-on-one fighting

bounce *(verb)* to leave, to exit a situation. *Variation:* **bizounce**

boys *(noun)* undercover cops

bribington, brib *(noun)* home, house. (Variation on *crib*, because members of the Bloods gang don't use the letter *c* in daily speech)

bugging *(verb)* acting dumb or silly

buns *(adjective)* scared to react

corny *(adjective)* trying to be cool, but not making it

cuffie smack *(verb phrase)* to knock someone's hat off

deep *(adjective)* 1. lost 2. very far away

dolo *(adjective)* physically alone, or solo

edumacation *(noun)* education

fall back *(verb phrase)* get off my back, step off, calm down

fresh *(adjective)* acknowledged by your peers as having money or having expensive clothing or appearance; recognized as cool

get stupid *(verb phrase)* show off your best dance moves. *Also,* **get saucy**

goonies *(noun)* friends, or people who will stand by you

get at me *(verb phrase)* embarrass me; make fun of me

get my lite feet going *(verb phrase)* to dance; *also*, to hurry up, to get away fast

guap *(noun)* a large amount of money

hater *(noun)* someone who does not like you

holla *(verb)* to acknowledge someone's presence; *also*, to indicate interest in hooking up with someone

hop off my swag *(verb phrase)* "Stop hating on me because I'm up there and you are not." Used disrespectfully.

hubby *(noun)* the boy you're in a relationship with. *Also,* **hubster**

kick rocks *(verb phrase)* get out of here, stop bothering me. *Also,* **kick rocks without socks**

kicks *(noun)* sneakers

let it rock *(verb phrase)* leave something alone in the moment, let something go

link me *(verb phrase)* call me; talk to me later. *Also,* **shout me**

make it hot *(verb phrase)* make it obvious, noticeable, to attract attention

merm *(noun)* Marmot-brand coat with pockets, targeted by thieves

muk *(adjective)* ugly

O.D. *(verb)* to overdo, *e.g.* "That teacher O.D.ing with the homework."

O.G. *(noun)* Original Gangster

GO ON TO NEXT PAGE

on point *(adjective phrase)* put together or done well (could describe, for example, a set of dance moves, an outfit that works, an argument for something)

pimp slap *(verb phrase)* to wind up, put your hand over the opposite shoulder, and whoosh, let free right into the person's face. *Also,* **box in the face**

play *(verb)* to mess around. Used with friends or people already known to you; *e.g.* "Why you playing so much?"

pop *(adjective)* 1. poor, having no money. 2. out of fashion.

pop off *(verb phrase)* fight me (invitation to fight)

rolling deep *(verb phrase)* having a lot of people with you

sell off *(adjective phrase)* trendy, fashionable, in style

sick *(adjective)* awesome, cool, interesting

smizzut *(noun)* slut

snuff *(verb)* to punch

swag *(noun)* superior social position

that don't rock *(verb phrase)* That's not good

tough *(adjective)* cool, looking good. *Also,* **hard**

tweaking (verb) 1. hallucinating; imagining things. 2. acting silly (synonym for **bugging**)

whack *(adjective)* boring; *also*, ridiculous

what it do *(verb phrase)* hi, what's up, what's happening. *Also,* **what it is**

wifey *(noun)* the girl you're in a relationship with

wilin out *(verb phrase)* acting in a wild or crazy manner. *Also* (when dancing) **get mad**

word *(verb)* that's right, I agree. *Also* **word up**

word up *(verb phrase)* a greeting, similar to "what's up"

word out *(verb phrase)* time to go, time to stop (opposite of the greeting **word up**)

yardie *(noun)* person from the Caribbean

yoke *(verb)* to pull someone up by the shoulders or neck, without inflicting pain; to shake someone up

GO ON TO NEXT PAGE

FOR DISCUSSION

FOR YOUTH

What words would you add to this dictionary based on common usage in your community? What words would you take out?

FOR ADULTS

Which colloquial words that you now routinely use first entered your vocabulary when you were a teenager? Do they still mean the same thing when used by youth today?

STOP
YOU HAVE
REACHED THE
END OF THIS
SECTION

Who's American?

P EOPLE OFTEN USE terms like "black" and "Latino" to cat-
egorize Bronx students. But students are more likely to
ask of a new acquaintance, "What are you?" Their black classmates may identify with Jamaica or Guinea or Nigeria or South
Carolina—or the Bronx. Their Latino classmates may be Mexi-
can or Dominican or Guatemalan—even if they were born in
the Bronx.

In this section, you will read ten responses in which students describe their family backgrounds. Questions 1–10 ask
you to infer from each description the student's own beliefs
about culture, ethnicity, or national allegiance.

Read the ten passages on the following pages, and answer the question that follows each passage. (A) (B) (C) (D)

ERIC | When people ask, "What are you?" you don't say, "I'm American." You say your heritage. I say I'm Puerto Rican, other people say Dominican, and so on, but we don't refer to ourselves as American.

1. Which statement best reflects Eric's view?

- (A) Puerto Ricans and Dominicans both come from the Caribbean, so they share a heritage.
- (B) Culture matters more than nationality.
- (C) Puerto Ricans aren't really American.
- (D) None of the above

JOSEFINA | When people ask me what I am, I say, "I'm Hispanic, but I was born here." I'm born in America, but I'm still Dominican, and Dominicans dance bachata and merengue and salsa. But I'm also half Panamanian, and we dance kumbi; my family taught me how to do it. When I go to a party and they play that, I feel good actually knowing how to dance it. I could be one of the only ones dancing. Nowadays, they play all kinds of music—and if I was only able to dance one type of music, I would feel weird. Being bicultural, you can listen to music or television from here and you can also listen to it from where you're from. You might feel closer to one, but you could switch back and forth, speak the language from here or the language from there. If you're with people from the Dominican Republic, you'll speak that way. And if you're with people from here, you'll speak another way.

2. Which statement best reflects Josefina's view?

- (A) You should only call yourself Hispanic if Spanish is your first language.
- (B) If you were born in America, you should call yourself American.
- (C) Every culture in your family can and should be a source of pride. You can call on each in its own context, and you have to learn to move easily among them.
- (D) None of the above

GO ON TO NEXT PAGE

IDALIA | My mom is an immigrant and she married a Mexican immigrant, and he has two kids here that are immigrants also. Actually, my stepfather broke up from his wife in Mexico when he came here, but he never really got a divorce, so now he can't get married because he could really get in trouble. It's hard—my mom has her green card, but her husband, he doesn't, so he has to always be careful what he does, because he could be sent back to Mexico. So my whole family, everybody that we live with, they're all immigrants. My brothers and I are the only Americans in the house, since we were all born here. And college is hard for immigrants. My stepfather's sister's daughter is going to college right now but because she's a Mexican, they don't give her financial aid. My mother was born in Panama, she came when she was two. She's a permanent resident, she went to college, but she didn't get no financial aid.

3. Which statement best reflects Idalia's view?

(A) As long as you're a legal immigrant, you have what you need in order to succeed in the United States.

(B) Even within one home, a family's individual members may fall into very different categories, which significantly affect their experiences of life in the United States.

(C) If you're American, then the others in your family are, too.

(D) All of the above

EFFE | I have brothers and sisters that live in Africa, they were born there to my father. Since the year 2000 we've been trying to get my oldest brother to come to America. He's trying to get to school so he can have a better life, because he's not doing so good over there. You have to pay a lot of money, for the documents and everything, and then my father has to go on interviews and show proof that he's his legal father. The thing that happened now, that's actually delaying us, is that we found out my brother is not really my brother. They took a DNA test, and my father's not really his father. So all of this money that my father paid to get him to come, and all the documents that he's been through, and everything that he's been doing for the past six years, has gone to waste. Now my brother or half-brother —whatever he is to me now—can't come to America, because we don't know who his father is, we don't know if his father is a citizen. All of his plans—everything has gone to dust, now!

4. Which statement best reflects Effe's view?

    (A) Legal immigration requirements do not always take into account the realities of familial attachments.

    (B) Once some family members get established in the United States, it's pretty easy for the others to follow.

    (C) Everyone from the extended family of an immigrant to the United States wants to come to America, too.

    (D) All of the above

GO ON TO NEXT PAGE ⇒

DINAH   Everybody came without papers, so it was very difficult for them to get jobs and everything like that. My mother had to do housecleaning, walking dogs, any kind of job she could get in order to support herself. She was 19, a college student, but my auntie had come up here a couple of years before, and my aunt told her to come up here and visit her. She was supposed to go back to Jamaica, but on your visa they give you a certain amount of time you can stay, and she overstayed, and if she went to Jamaica, it would be impossible for her to come back. So she stayed in America and met my father.

5. Which statement best reflects Dinahs view?

- (A) Immigrants get to the United States any way they can, then stay on, hoping to beat the immigration system.
- (B) Opportunities are always better in the United States than in other countries.
- (C) A person may have immigrated to the U.S. as much by accident as by intention.
- (D) None of the above

DEBBIE | I have a green card, but I am not an American, and I don't want to be an American! I like the country, and I think the country has a lot to offer me—that's why I'm here. But personally, I love my country, I love where I'm from like crazy. I miss where I'm from, crazy. And I don't have much fun here. I think I'd have a lot more fun where I was born, but I think I just have a lot more opportunities here. There's a lot more educational opportunities here, jobs . . .

6. Which statement best reflects Debbie's view?

- (A) Getting the green card is the first step on the road to the American dream.
- (B) Practical and emotional factors compete in an immigrant's attitudes toward the new country.
- (C) Immigrants come to the United States to escape miserable conditions in their home countries.
- (D) None of the above

GO ON TO NEXT PAGE

ADEYEFA | Legally, I am American, but I come from African descent. There are three generations since my family came from Africa. To be an American is to have advantages, get all the opportunities here, find truer happiness and all that other stuff. I don't like to be labeled "African-American," because that's like putting "I'm an American" before "I'm an African." So that's why I like to say I'm a African, born in America. I'm African heritage first. I'm from Nigeria. My father is an African priest, he studies the religion of Oitungee, the oldest African tribe. So there's a lot of African things we do in our house. I learn how to drum, and I learn African dancing, and cooking, and a lot of African culture.

7. Which statement best reflects Adeyefa's view?

- (A) How you name your culture is important, because it makes a statement about how you live.
- (B) Hyphenating your ethnic identification is the best way to express your cultural allegiances.
- (C) To call yourself an African, you should have been born in Africa.
- (D) None of the above

SEAN

My father is Cherokee Indian, and his father was African-American. My mom is Jamaican, but I don't say I'm Jamaican, because I'm not! I was born here, so I say I'm American. Sometimes when they ask me on paper, I say I'm African-American, because that's the only place they have. My great-grandmother was Cherokee Indian, and my great-grandfather was half Cherokee Indian and half black. And my grandmother is half Cherokee Indian and half African-American. She has a Indian name and all that. But I don't get involved in all that stuff. I could, if I wanted to! But I'm not going to do it and I'm not going to be true to it. I don't have the time to.

8. Which statement best reflects Sean's view?

- (A) In order to represent yourself as part of a culture, it's important to have the time and interest to learn about it.
- (B) If you look black and you are an American citizen, you are African-American.
- (C) Five choices as to race and ethnicity on the U.S. census form are enough to represent most Americans.
- (D) All of the above

GO ON TO NEXT PAGE

CRYSTAL | I consider myself black. Because both of my parents is from the South. People from down there, they consider people as just being black—as in "nothing else." No Dominican, no Spanish, no nothing, no mix, just black. My parents come from South Carolina. I really don't know when they came up here. When people ax me, I say I'm black, I don't say nothing else.

9. Which statement best reflects Crystal's's view?

    (A) African heritage is the primary cultural identification of African-Americans.

    (B) People are largely going to identify you by the color of your skin, not by your ethnicity.

    (C) America is color blind.

    (D) None of the above

> DINAH Everybody in my family has some kind of different race. So I can't say, I'm just black, I'm just white, I'm just Chinese, I'm just Venezuelan. I'm everything! I was born here, so I am an American by law, but I don't consider myself as an American. I put myself in every category. I'm a little bit of you, I'm a little bit of everything! If someone said, "Are you Dominican?"—I have some, somewhere!

10. Which statement best reflects Dinah's view?

   A The United States is more of a melting pot today than it ever was before.
   B You should identify yourself as whatever ethnicity makes up the greatest part of your gene pool.
   C Even when someone is born in the U.S., the term "American" does not convey the richness of the person's cultural heritage.
   D All of the above

GO ON TO NEXT PAGE

ANSWER
KEY

1. A **B** C D

2. A B **C** D

3. A **B** C D

4. **A** B C D

5. A B **C** D

6. A **B** C D

7. **A** B C D

8. **A** B C D

9. A **B** C D

10. A B **C** D

FOR DISCUSSION

FOR YOUTH

> When people use terms like "black," "Latino," or "American" to identify you, what parts of your identity might they be leaving out?

> How does your ethnic background affect you at school? Can you suggest ways to bring aspects or strengths of your culture'into the classroom?

FOR ADULTS

> Based on the passages in this section, how is the definition of "family" affected by biography and geography among students in the Bronx? Among students in your own classroom?

> What resources and strengths might be overlooked in a multicultural classroom? How might those resources and strengths affect how students relate to school?

STOP
YOU HAVE
REACHED THE
END OF THIS
SECTION

Why Do We Fight?

I N THIS SECTION, Bronx students describe their different philosophies on when to take part in a fight, and why.

After each philosophy, you will read a scenario in which the student describes a possibly hostile interaction. To answer the test questions, you will have to think about what priorities drive this particular student's response. Does the student need to establish a reputation of strength? To release stress? To ensure personal safety? To show loyalty to friends?

The multiple-choice answers and the answer key in this section are written by Bronx students. If you do not understand their colloquial language, turn for help to Section 1, "Words You'll Need for the Test" (pages 5–9).

→ Scenes from Our Days

> *Read the passages on the following pages, and answer the question that follows each passage.* Ⓐ Ⓑ Ⓒ Ⓓ

DINAH | Some people fight to boost their popularity, so they can be known throughout the school as "Don't mess with her, she'll beat you up." That's how I got my rep up, because I used to fight a lot, and I used to win most of the fights. In the 'hood, if you're tough and you beat people up, you have the respect of others. I'm not gonna let somebody curse me out and not say nothing back. If I wouldn't do anything, one, they would jump me. Two, I would be looked on at school like I was a wuss. I would get no respect. That's just not who I am.

ɪ. Things are building up at school and at home. Dinah is having a bad day, and she's got a lot on her mind as she walks home from school. As a prank—or maybe as part of a gang initiation—someone she doesn't know comes from the side and snuffs her in the face. In which of the following ways is Dinah likely to respond?

Ⓐ She calls up her friends.
Ⓑ She starts punching him without hesitation.
Ⓒ She says, "That's your life, 'cause my pops is a triple OG."
Ⓓ She stops to think, and then decides to hit back.

> **ADEYEFA** As long as they don't touch you, you don't have nothing to fight for, so just walk away. Words don't hurt me, so I don't really care. If it gets to the point where you put your hands on me, then I'm going to defend myself. But you only fight to subdue your opponent, so that they can't hurt you or anyone. If someone was picking on a friend for no apparent reason, I would help him out. But if it was a situation that was pointless to fight over, I wouldn't bother with it. It's not my problem, it's your problem. If you're my friend, don't put me in a situation where I'm gonna get harmed. Don't mess my future up.

2. Adeyefa is with his friend Robert on Robert's birthday. Another friend comes up to start giving Robert his "birthday punches," but seems to be punching him with too much force. Robert asks the friend to stop, but he doesn't. Then Adeyefa warns the friend to chill, but he keeps punching. In which of the following ways is Adeyefa likely to respond?

    (A) He beats the living daylights out of the puncher.
    (B) He walks away.
    (C) He scraps with the puncher, but only to a level.
    (D) He yokes the puncher up and says, "That don't rock!"

GO ON TO NEXT PAGE

CARLOS | If there was a problem with somebody, I would try to talk it out with them, I wouldn't just start cursing out, because that's just not the way. But if I was caught in a situation where somebody's gonna hit me, of course I'm gonna have to defend myself. I can't just stand there and say, "No it's okay, sorry, stop." It's not realistic. I guess I'd have to hit back, if they're hitting me. You're not gonna just walk away. It's not only about respect, it's also self-defense.

3. Carlos is leaving school with his friend Wilson, when one of Wilson's haters comes up and says, "I got you later!" After he leaves, Wilson turns to Carlos and says, "You got my back, right?" In which of the following ways is Carlos likely to respond?

    A Because Wilson's hater has seen them together, Carlos decides to help defend Wilson later.

    B He and Wilson chase after the hater and wash him up.

    C He chills with Wilson for the rest of the afternoon, talking about how to handle the situation.

    D He bounces, because it's not really his problem.

DINAH | Our school is on the second floor of a big building in the Bronx, but we don't know everybody in the building. Students from the schools on the other floors sometimes show up in our halls to see their friends, even though they're not supposed to, and we all see each other on the streets. So you have to have your own group, that's going to be loyal to you just like you're loyal to them. And if you have a problem with someone from another group, news is going to get around to the whole community, inside and outside of school. Depending on how you handle the situation, you either gain respect or you lose all respect—outside your group and also within your group.

4. Dinah walks out of English class into the hallway and another student steps on her newly purchased Jordans. The smart way for her to react is:

A. Continue on to math class without saying anything. The other girl probably didn't mean any harm.

B. Glare at the other student and continue on to class. Dinah can't just let that go unnoticed.

C. Grab the other student's bookbag and throw it to the floor, and then call her a punk. Continue to class before a teacher can get involved.

D. Pull the other student into the stairwell to avoid the surveillance cameras and then punch her in the face.

GO ON TO NEXT PAGE

ANSWER KEY

I. (A) **B** (C) (D)

Explanation: *From Dinah's perspective, if she hesitates she is lost.*

2. (A) (B) **C** (D)

Explanation: *Adeyefa will use force now, but only to the point that the puncher stops attacking his friend. If he yokes him up and threatens him, he's inviting a bigger conflict later, when the puncher returns with his friends.*

3. (A) (B) **C** (D)

Explanation: *Carlos likes to think over whatever situation he's in, before he takes any action.*

4. (A) **B** (C) (D)

Explanation: *When Dinah glares at her, that means: "You want to really see somebody that's up there? You want to see somebody that's got people? You want to see somebody that's just better than you? All right. I got you later."*

FOR DISCUSSION

FOR YOUTH

> Make a list of what students have to do in your school to earn the respect of peers. Then list what students have to do to earn the respect of adults. Does any example appear on both lists? If not, why?

> In your school, how do students resolve conflicts among themselves? Outside school hours, do they resolve conflicts differently?

> What ways does your school provide for students to relieve stress? To gain the recognition and respect of peers?

FOR ADULTS

> In what settings could you best listen to youth, to learn how and why students react differently in moments of stress? How might you act on the insights they gain?

> What might students' speech, posture, clothing, and other "status markers" have to do with their personal safety?

> What school structures might help urban high school students build a reputation of strength, release stress, gain recognition, and maintain an acceptable social standing, without resorting to violence?

STOP
YOU HAVE
REACHED THE
END OF THIS
SECTION

How Do You Get There?

T HIS SECTION ASKS YOU to make some of the same cost-benefit calculations that Bronx students do, as they travel to and from school, work, and after-school programs.

To answer the questions, you will first need to understand the system that New York City Transit uses when it gives some students free or reduced-price fare cards on the bus and subway system. Next, several scenarios will describe different students' transportation choices. You will be asked to analyze the time and money factors that will result in the best outcome for each case.

Student Public Transit Discounts in New York City

At the beginning of each semester, each school distributes student Metrocards to its students, so they can travel to and from school and after-school activities. Without student Metrocards, one trip on the subway or bus is a $2 fare. Student Metrocards come with these limitations:

> Students who live within half a mile of their school receive no student Metrocard. Regardless of where their after-school programs may be, they have no access to free transportation.

> Students who live more than 1.5 miles from school receive a full-fare student Metrocard. This allows three trips each day, which means they can go from home to school (1 trip), from school to a job or after-school activity (1 trip), and then back home (1 trip). Each such trip may include one transfer: bus to bus, or bus to subway. They do not, for example, have the option of taking a bus in the Bronx, transferring to a subway into Manhattan, then transferring to a crosstown bus.

> Students who live between .5 and 1.5 miles from school receive a half-fare student Metrocard. However, they can only use it on the bus, as subway turnstiles have no mechanism for collecting the remaining half-fare of $1 each trip. If they take the bus to and from school (e.g., to arrive on time, to shelter from bad weather, or to avoid a walk through a dangerous neighborhood), these students pay $10 a week to get to and from school. If they take the subway to school, they must pay full fare, which requires them to buy an additional Metrocard.

→ The Difference One Block Makes

Read the Rider Information on the opposite page and answer Questions 1 and 2 based on the facts in "the situation."

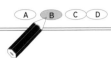

THE SITUATION

Destiny and Precious live near the E. 170th Street stop on the D subway line in the Bronx. Destiny lives just under 1.5 miles from school, and gets a half-fare student Metrocard. Precious lives one block from Destiny, just over 1.5 miles from the school, so her Metrocard is free for 3 trips daily. They usually meet at the bus stop to take the public bus to school. On Monday through Friday, both girls work for 4 hours after school at a Burger King on 42nd Street and 7th Avenue in Manhattan. They have several choices for how to get from school to their after-school jobs and then back home:

> The 2 subway line from school to work (46 minutes)
> The bus from school to work (1 hour 21 minutes, in ideal traffic)
> The D subway from work to home (37 minutes)
> The express bus from work to home (61 minutes, in ideal traffic)

1. If Destiny uses her half-fare Metrocard to get to and from work, thereby saving money but limiting herself to the bus, while Precious uses the subway, what is the difference in hours per week the two girls devote to holding down their after-school jobs?

- A Destiny devotes 9 hours and 30 minutes more than Precious
- B Destiny devotes 7 hours and 40 minutes more than Precious
- C Destiny and Precious devote the same time
- D Precious devotes 5 hours and 15 minutes less than Destiny

GO ON TO NEXT PAGE

2. If Destiny decides to take the subway to and from work, thereby losing the benefits of her half-fare Metrocard, which of the following statements best describes the difference in the two girls' finances at the end of the week? (Both girls are paid minimum wage, $7.15 an hour.)

    A Destiny will have spent $10 more for transit than Precious did.

    B When you deduct from Destiny's earnings the money she had to spend on transit, Precious will have pocketed $71.50 more than Destiny.

    C Destiny will have spent 14 percent more of her earnings on transit than Precious did.

    D None of the above.

4

→ Insufficient Fare

Answer Questions 3 and 4 based on calculating the costs for each student in the situation described below.

THE SITUATION | Jose, Hector, and Winston, all students at Bronx Leadership Academy II, share an interest in dance, writing, and singing. Jose lives 2 miles from the school, Hector lives .75 miles from the school, and Winston lives two short blocks from the school. A friend tells them about a nonprofit organization that brings diverse students together across school districts, to create musical theater based on their own lives. Rehearsals take place on the Upper East Side of Manhattan, three days a week after school, for 24 weeks per year.

To get to this program from their school, the boys can either take the 21 bus to the 5 train (travel time: 45 minutes), or walk to the Bx15 bus and transfer to the M15 bus (travel time: 1 hour). Use the space below to find the weekly travel costs for each option and student. Then answer Questions 3 and 4.

OPTION 1: 21 bus to the 5 train

Weekly cost for Jose: $___.___

Weekly cost for Hector: $___.___

Weekly cost for Winston: $___.___

OPTION 2: B15 bus to the M15 bus

Weekly cost for Jose: $___.___

Weekly cost for Hector: $___.___

Weekly cost for Winston: $___.___

REMEMBER

▶ Students who live within .5 miles of their school receive no student Metrocard. They pay the regular $2 fare for bus or subway.

▶ Students who live between .5 and 1.5 miles from school receive a half-fare Metrocard, but it's only good for the bus. On subways they pay the full $2 fare.

▶ Students who live more than 1.5 miles from school receive a full-fare Metrocard.

▶ Transfers are free from subway-to-bus, bus-to-bus, and bus-to-subway (one per trip).

GO ON TO NEXT PAGE

3. Using Option 1, who pays the least?

- Ⓐ Jose
- Ⓑ Hector
- Ⓒ Winston

4. Using Option 2, who pays the most?

- Ⓐ Jose
- Ⓑ Hector
- Ⓒ Winston

5. At the end of the 24-week theater program, how much more time will Hector have spent getting from school to the program and home than his best friend Jose spent—if Hector decides to save money and use only the bus, while Jose uses the subway-bus combination?

- Ⓐ Hector will have spent 12.5 hours more than Jose.
- Ⓑ Hector will have spent 18 hours more than Jose.
- Ⓒ Hector will have spent 14.25 hours more than Jose.
- Ⓓ None of the above.

ANSWER
KEY

1. (A) ●B● (C) (D)

Explanation: *Destiny spends 35 minutes more than Precious getting from school to work every day, and 57 minutes more than Precious getting home from work. This amounts to 7 hours and 40 minutes more time than Precious spends on her job every week.*

2. (A) ●B● (C) (D)

Explanation: *Destiny spends 14 percent of her earnings ($20, or 5 round-trip subway fares at $2 each, out of her $143 before-tax wages) on transit, while Precious spends nothing.*

3. ●A● (B) (C)

Explanation: *Jose spends nothing on travel costs, as he lives more than 1.5 miles from his school and thus gets a free full-fare Metrocard.*

4. (A) (B) ●C●

Explanation: *Winston lives within .5 miles of school and must pay full fare, or $12 weekly.*

5. (A) (B) (C) ●D●

Explanation: *At the end of the 24-week program, Hector will have spent 46 more hours getting to and from the program than Jose spent, in order to save money.*

GO ON TO NEXT PAGE

FOR DISCUSSION

FOR YOUTH

> How do you get to school and to your after-school activities? How much does that cost you? Do you think that cost is fair? Can you suggest other possibilities?

> What public body sets the policies that affect student transportation in your city or town?

FOR ADULTS

> What factors might motivate urban students who live within a half-hour's walk of school to take public transit instead?

> At your school, to what extent might students' tardiness result from their transportation options?

STOP
YOU HAVE
REACHED THE
END OF THIS
SECTION

The Recruitment Decision

T HIS SECTION PRESENTS a dialogue among seven Bronx students about the pros and cons of enlisting in the armed forces. One student is on the brink of his decision, and each of his six companions contributes a perspective to the conversation.

After each passage, you will be asked questions that test your comprehension of the issues and viewpoints that emerge through the students' conversation.

→ Becoming a Target

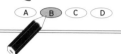

After reading what students say in each of the passages that follow, answer Questions 1–8.

FOR REFERENCE

> The current size of the enlisted military force is 1.2 million. Each year, approximately 200,000 new recruits are needed to maintain this level.

> The Department of Defense is the largest employer in the United States.

> An estimated 4.4 million youth will turn 18 and be eligible for enlistment in 2009.

> Black and Hispanic groups have lower enlistment rates than whites, with Hispanics showing higher rates than blacks.

> The ethnic distribution of the U.S. armed forces is 62 percent white, 20 percent black, and 11 percent Hispanic. In contrast, the general population of youth age 18-24 is 65 percent white, 14 percent black, and 15 percent Hispanic.

> The military services are 18 percent female, compared with 51 percent female in the general civilian population of the same age.

> The proportion of high school males indicating that they "definitely will" join a military service declined from 12 to 8 percent from the mid-1980s to 2005.

DONIVAN | The other day I was over on Third Avenue. The guys come over there with their girlfriends when they get their nails done, and we sit outside the nail salon and wait. On the other side there's a recruitment center—when you come to the Bronx, you see them all over the place. When they spot you, they come tap you on your shoulder and ask you a bunch of questions. And the Navy recruiter was trying to recruit me to join. He says, "I'm interested in your future—basically, you'll be set for life. You should think about it. We should exchange numbers." So he called me all the time, just to see if I was interested.

TRAVIS | They target males that look like they ain't doing nothing with their life. They target them and try to better their lives, so they say. An Army recruiter had came to my friend, and asked him how old he was. He said 22. He said, "You finish high school?" He said, "No." He said, "Well you could go join the Army or Navy, and then we'll get you through school and better your life." And two or three days later, he was part of the Army.

1. With which statement would both Donivan and Travis agree?

   (A) The recruiter cares about their future.
   (B) The military offers them a much brighter future than staying in the Bronx.
   (C) The recruiter is targeting young men like them.
   (D) The recruiter will give them plenty of time to make their decision.

GO ON TO NEXT PAGE

DONIVAN | The first thing they ask you is "Do you plan to go to college?" They see that as the first thing that you'll probably be interested in. And then they'll talk about, "Oh, what are you interested in?" And then after that they'll go into an in-depth talk about how they can do so many things for you. They'll pay you such and such to go to college. They'll give you a stipend. I told my mom about it, and I told her it would be a way for me to pay for college.

MARKEDIA | I think that the message they sending out is, how the government and whoever takes in charge of the military, they think poorly of us. That we need the government to help us. So they come to the people who's not highly richer than the white people, the rich people out there. They saying that they giving us a better chance for life. I think they think that we lower than them.

2. Donivan finds the recruiter's interest in him to be:

 (A) Genuine—he sees Donivan's potential and wants to help him pursue his interests.
 (B) Condescending—he assumes Donivan has no other choices.
 (C) Self-serving—he's not really interested in Donivan's college education.
 (D) Helpful—whatever his reasons are, a stipend for college is involved.

3. Which of the choices in Question 2 would Markedia agree with?

5

DONIVAN | I saw a commercial, and it was a father and a son. The picture was kind of catchy. It showed a guy excelling in what he was doing in life. The son had just came home from the war or something. And the father's, like, "You're a changed man, you looking me in the eye now, you never used to do that before." Everybody want to strengthen their life somehow.

DINAH | It may give you a certain type of discipline but that's not the type of discipline that I believe in. It's more the boot camp-ish, you know, discipline. But I believe in the more natural discipline. I don't know how to explain it, but it's like I believe in home training, not that you have to go out somewhere else to get training.

4. If Dinah saw the commercial that Donivan saw, she would most likely think that:

    A Core values and discipline come from one's home and family.
    B The military uses slick marketing techniques to exploit young men's need for approval from their fathers.
    C A good reason to join the military is to make your family proud.
    D Joining the military helps a young person grow up.

GO ON TO NEXT PAGE

DONIVAN | The Army, they kill a lot of people daily, so that was out of the question. I can't live with myself knowing I killed somebody for unreasonable cause. In the Navy, they don't do that much fighting. They fight when it's necessary, when we're needed. And the Navy's not really always needed. Navy's really more for homefront, repairing stuff, fixing ships. You're doing for others, you're not doing for yourself. When I realized that I fit every requirement, and where I wanted to see myself in four years, the Navy was going to be able to help me with it.

TRAVIS | I don't want to be a part of any of that stuff. I ain't trying to kill nobody. Poor like me—not necessarily poor, but in a struggle like me. But they struggle is way worse. We both—everybody—trying to survive. You're putting yourself on the line, going to another country who's doing way worse than this, that's how I see it. We shooting people with rags. I don't really know the reasons, I hear a lot of purposes on TV. For me, that's not good enough.

5. Travis and Donivan would agree that:

A If you join the military, you're going to be killing people.
B Military service is a force for good in the world.
C The government has good reasons for its military actions.
D Helping out people in need is a noble act.

DINAH | Two particular women in my building, that joined, they came back. One, she's looking good now, she just got married, and she's working as a police officer. The other one joined because her father died in the military. She wanted to fulfill his dreams, so to say, she was young when she joined. She never knew what the outcome was gonna be, but now she regrets that she went there. She came back, she's still living with her mother, and her life is, like, ruined. She has no job, she just lives so poor. I've never seen anything like that in my life.

6. With which statement would Dinah most likely agree?

- (A) The military will continue to support you after your term of service.
- (B) There's no guarantee that your life will improve as a result of joining the military.
- (C) The skills you learn in the military can help you build a successful career once you return to civilian life.
- (D) If you can't get your life together when you finish your military service, it's your own fault.

DONIVAN | I seen my recruiter two weeks ago, he talked to me. The next day he called my house, asked for me, told me to come in and sign the papers. The next day he came to pick me up from my house to take me to go take the test. They make sure everything is done so they don't have back-paperwork. They very consistently up on you, to make sure everything is situated.

DEBBIE | I think that a lot of people don't have time to do the research. Because when you walking on the road and they approach you and they say, "Oh we're recruiting for the Army or Navy," they just hit you with all that good stuff right then and there. And then they might pull out a paper and ask you to sign it. So you don't even have time to go to your house to go look up on the Internet the bad effects of war or whatever. So that's why a lot of people probably don't even know the knowledge that they need to know, going into the Army.

7. Donivan and Debbie would agree that:

- (A) The recruiter is determined to sign up new recruits quickly.
- (B) The recruiter will help Donivan to thoroughly consider his decision to enlist.
- (C) The recruiter is trying to pressure young people into signing up.
- (D) The recruiter's efficient approach helps Donivan make his decision in an adult manner.

8. Considering all the passages you have read in Section 5, choose which of the following people would be most likely to give Donivan insightful and unbiased advice about his enlistment decision:

- A His high school guidance counselor, who has a caseload of 500 students.
- B His military recruiter, whose sworn duty is to represent the military of the United States, and who has specific recruiting targets to meet that month in order to fulfill his job requirements.
- C His mother, a head of household who works two jobs and has no savings for her son's college education.
- D His friends.

GO ON TO NEXT PAGE

ANSWER
KEY

1. Ⓐ Ⓑ ●C Ⓓ

2. Ⓐ Ⓑ Ⓒ ●D

3. Ⓐ ●B Ⓒ Ⓓ

4. ●A Ⓑ Ⓒ Ⓓ

5. Ⓐ Ⓑ Ⓒ ●D

6. Ⓐ ●B Ⓒ Ⓓ

7. ●A Ⓑ Ⓒ Ⓓ

8. Ⓐ Ⓑ Ⓒ ●D

FOR DISCUSSION

→ Rank the following priorities in Donivan's decision to enlist:

 # Donivan's Priority

___ Self-discipline
___ Respect of friends and family
___ Educational and career opportunities
___ Patriotism
___ Knowing the reasons behind current military actions

▸ **FOR YOUTH**

> Describe your own experiences, if any, with military recruiters.

> Have you considered enlisting in the military? Why or why not?

▸ **FOR ADULTS**

> What opportunities does your school provide for students to discuss the pros and cons of military service, without recruiters present?

> What critical thinking skills does the enlistment decision require of youth? Do you see those skills in the students' words presented in this section? In the discussions by your own students about this subject?

STOP
YOU HAVE REACHED THE END OF THIS SECTION

What to Take To College

Tʜɪs ꜱᴇᴄᴛɪᴏɴ ᴘʀᴇꜱᴇɴᴛꜱ the thinking of Bronx students as they work out their ideas about where to attend college, by speaking about what will help them do well there.

Each student approaches that subject with an individual mix of temperament, personal and academic experiences, attitudes and habits, social relationships, and expectations (both their own and those of others). Based on your reading of passages by individual students, Questions 1 through 4 ask you to assess the impact those various factors may have on their future college success.

→ The Big Decision

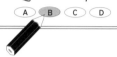

After reading what students say in each of the passages that follow, answer Questions 1–4.

DEBBIE   Maybe it's a matter of not being comfortable. Because a person performs in their comfort zone. When I'm around people of my own ethnicity, or race, or gender, or whatever, I tend to feel more comfortable. I fit in better with them, so as a result, I produce to my ability. If a person is comfortable where they're at, I think they're mostly likely to achieve their full potential. But if you're in an environment where you're not comfortable, you're not going to achieve what needs to be done.

---

1. Which of the following statements best represents Debbie's position?

    Ⓐ When given a real academic challenge, disadvantaged students will rise to increased achievement.

    Ⓑ Black students perform better at historicaally black colleges and universities.

    Ⓒ Strong social relationships among students have an important positive effect on academic learning.

    Ⓓ Students will only succeed in college if they can learn to perform outside their comfort zones.

JOSEFINA | You're also going to need friends. I was slacking off last year, and I started talking to smarter people—and I was like, "Okay, if she could do it, then I could do it, too." The people you're surrounded by, they're helping you move on too, because they give you confidence. Once I'm in college, they can help me too, [if you go to college together]. You're already accustomed to those people and you're thinking positive while you're going to college—you're like, "Okay, I'm gonna do it," and you do it, as a group.

2. At which kind of college would Josefina need the support of her friends in order to thrive?

- (A) A large public university in her own city.
- (B) A diverse state university in another state.
- (C) A private liberal arts college where she receives a special scholarship for minority students.
- (D) All of the above.

GO ON TO NEXT PAGE

GENESIS But I don't think going to college with friends is that good an idea. I've heard of many stories of kids that go to college with their friends and all their priorities go out the window. They just start partying and thinking about having fun, and not focusing on what's at hand. It's good to have support, but it's also good to decide for yourself—you don't want to base your decisions on what somebody else has because they feel is right. You have to look inside yourself and say, "For me, that might be the correct thing." Just because it looks good while they talk about it, it just might be their vision, but mine has to be different.

3. Based on this passage, what kind of support would most help Genesis during her first year away from home at a demanding college?

- (A) "Care packages" and cards from her family during exams.
- (B) Frequent phone calls and text messages from her friends at home.
- (C) Joining a sorority on campus.
- (D) None of the above.

DINAH   I think in a more mixed environment, black people tend to do worse, because of the way people see different types of people in society. Like they always say Chinese people's good with doing math, and white people are supposed to be better at reading and stuff. And when black people come in that environment and they see "these people are good at this, these people are good at that," they feel like "OK, what are we good at?" Everybody thinks that all black people are good at playing basketball or football, and not good at academics. So when they're faced into an environment with academics, they're going to feel like "OK, I'm not supposed to be good at this." It's going to bring down their pride, bring down everything that they believe in, that they work for. And it's going to allow them to do worse, because they gonna feel like they're not gonna be able to match up with everybody, because of what society believes each race does.

4. Which of the following statements best represents Dinah's position?

    (A) Chinese people have an advantage because their culture pushes them to excel in math.

    (B) More than for other ethnic groups, racism and prejudice negatively affect the academic achievement of black students.

    (C) If you have pride in your ethnic or racial identity, other people's expectations will not affect your ability to succeed academically.

    (D) All of the above.

GO ON TO NEXT PAGE

ANSWER
KEY

1. Ⓐ Ⓑ **Ⓒ** Ⓓ

Explanation: *For Debbie, feeling comfortable in her social context is a prerequisite for success.*

2. Ⓐ Ⓑ Ⓒ **Ⓓ**

Explanation: *A student like Josefina gains confidence in any demanding academic situation from seeing other students like herself do well. Without a supportive peer group, Josefina might feel lost in a large school and intimidated at a mostly white school.*

3. **Ⓐ** Ⓑ Ⓒ Ⓓ

Explanation: *Genesis is determined to focus on academics and wants to avoid too many social distractions. But she will need others to show their support as she faces academic challenges.*

4. Ⓐ **Ⓑ** Ⓒ Ⓓ

Explanation: *Dinah points out the particular challenge that black students face from racism and prejudice in the academic setting.*

FOR DISCUSSION

FOR YOUTH

What kind of college do you want to go to? What kind of academic and social supports will you need once you are there?

FOR ADULTS

Aside from academic preparation, what supports can educators provide to help students thrive once in college?

STOP
YOU HAVE REACHED THE END OF THIS SECTION

What Is Intelligent?

T HIS SECTION WILL TEST your ability to observe what
counts as "smart" in the world of a Bronx public high
school student.

First, you will match up students' own descriptions of
intelligent behavior with some of the criteria that educators use
in assessing intelligence.

Next, you will be asked to apply the students' perspectives
on intelligence to fictitious scenarios involving behavior in or
out of school.

As you work, be sure to notice the differences among the
opinions that students express about intelligence. If you do not
understand the colloquial language in this section, turn for
help to Section 1, "Words You'll Need for the Test."

You are using higher order thinking skills when

> You can recall information
> You can analyze a situation
> You can make comparisons
> You can speculate or make an inference
> You can judge or evaluate

The skill of code-switching involves choosing which language or dialect to use depending on the social context of an interaction or conversation.

The theory of multiple intelligences proposes that a person shows "intelligence" through any of a wide array of abilities, including linguistic, logical-mathematical, spatial, bodily-kinesthetic, musical, interpersonal, intrapersonal, and naturalistic.

→ Which
Theory
Fits?

Read the Reference section on the opposite page, then select the academic idea that best matches each student's ideas about intelligence as stated in the passages that follow. Ⓐ Ⓑ Ⓒ Ⓓ

1. Saying someone "has intelligence"—it's too elaborate to put in one box. There's different kinds of smart. There's outside smart, there's vocabulary smart . . . there's so many different kinds of smart that you just can't say, "Oh, he's smart" for this reason and only this reason. (Sean)

    Ⓐ Higher order thinking skills
    Ⓑ Code-switching
    Ⓒ Multiple intelligences
    Ⓓ None of the above

2. Inside a more uptight environment like school or a job interview, I would expect a smart person to be using proper grammar, not to act like they're in a 'hood environment. When we're outside, though, you have to fit in with the crowd. If you don't, then people are not going to see you as street smart; they're going to see you as *only* book smart. (Dinah)

    Ⓐ Higher order thinking skills
    Ⓑ Code-switching
    Ⓒ Multiple intelligences
    Ⓓ None of the above

GO ON TO NEXT PAGE

3. It could be the smallest thing. A person getting a CD, if they start thinking about it, might not want to start listening to explicit content. If they go get something to eat, go get clothing, they might think about "What am I gonna use these clothes for? Is it going to be appropriate for this situation?" or "Will this food help me in the long run?"(Genesis)

- (A) Higher order thinking skills
- (B) Code-switching
- (C) Multiple intelligences
- (D) None of the above

→ Whose
Actions Are
Intelligent?

On the basis of the following descriptions of students, decide whether each student is showing "intelligence."

4. At 14, Manuel immigrated from Guatemala to the Bronx with his mother and siblings, after his father disappeared. In ninth grade he is pulled out for an extra ESL class, but he failed all his other classes for the first two marking periods. He is only slowly catching up in this new school, where he struggles to understand not just the English of his teacher but even the Spanish of his Dominican and Puerto Rican classmates. The oldest in his family, he is the one who makes doctor appointments for his mother and translates the directions on her insulin shots. He doesn't tell her about parent conferences, because he doesn't want to worry her about his poor grades, but about once a week he stays after school, making his ten-year-old sister wait while he gets extra help in reading. By year's end, Manuel is passing all his classes, but just barely, and he talks freely in Spanish with the other students.

Is Manuel showing "intelligence"?

- Ⓐ No, his year-end grades show that he is probably not spending enough time on schoolwork.
- Ⓑ Yes, but only in situations where he can speak Spanish.
- Ⓒ No, he should not be speaking Spanish during school hours.
- Ⓓ Yes, he is dealing with many complex situations that require critical thinking.
- Ⓔ All of the above.

GO ON TO NEXT PAGE ⇒

5. Joseph, an eleventh grader, comes to class on time and dresses appropriately. His parents both work, but they're usually home for dinner with him, and they come to parent conferences. He turns his homework in on time and does well on in-class tests. However, he is very awkward in social situations. He doesn't mingle with the troublemakers, but he also doesn't seem to have any friends.

Is Joseph showing "intelligence"?

- (A) Yes, he's going to get good grades and get into college.
- (B) No, he's asking to be picked on by his schoolmates.
- (C) Yes, he's staying away from bad influences.
- (D) No, he lacks interpersonal intelligence, which is the key to success in life.
- (E) All of the above.

6. As soon as Delia turned 16, she applied for a job at the public library branch near the school, so she could buy the clothes she wants in order to look fresh. She likes the job because it's easy to do homework during the slow times, and even though she works 20 hours a week she can still keep her grades up. By spring, she is dressing very sharp, and she has saved enough to go on a trip to visit colleges. One day she gets to the library early and is playing around with friends on the steps when her supervisor passes by and hears her say, "I'ma cuffie smack you, hater!" When Delia checks in a few minutes later, he comments, "I didn't recognize you out there, Delia—I've never heard you talk that way before!"

Is Delia showing "intelligence"?

- (A) Yes, she knows how to adapt to a variety of social contexts.
- (B) Yes, but it's not smart to hang out with those kids before work.
- (C) No, she shouldn't have let her boss catch her playing outside of work.
- (D) None of the above.

GO ON TO NEXT PAGE

ANSWER
KEY

1. Ⓐ Ⓑ **Ⓒ** Ⓓ

2. Ⓐ **Ⓑ** Ⓒ Ⓓ

3. **Ⓐ** Ⓑ Ⓒ Ⓓ

4. Ⓐ Ⓑ Ⓒ **Ⓓ**

Explanation: *Manuel is dealing skillfully with many complex situations that involve ranking priorities and other critical thinking. Much of what he is doing so successfully is not seen or acknowledged at school, but his family and peers can see it.*

5. Ⓐ Ⓑ Ⓒ Ⓓ **Ⓔ**

Explanation: *Joseph is gifted at the areas rewarded by schools, and he has enough support to achieve at his ability level in those areas. He will no doubt get good grades, but unless he improves his Bronx survival skills he may struggle in his high school years.*

6. Ⓐ Ⓑ Ⓒ **Ⓓ**

Explanation: *School matters to Delia and she knows how to plan ahead. She also has the ability to negotiate different social situations, behaving appropriately for each one as it comes.*

FOR DISCUSSION

FOR YOUTH

> What do you do that's "smart" that your teachers might not understand?

> Describe a person or situation that made you feel intelligent. Has there ever been a person or situation that made you feel not intelligent? Have those experiences affected your actions since then? If so, describe how.

FOR ADULTS

In an urban high school setting, students know that many different eyes and ears are assessing them at once.

> To survive and thrive, what factors must they take into consideration?

> What higher-order thinking skills must they use?

STOP
YOU HAVE
REACHED THE
END OF THIS
SECTION

Who Should Take This Test?

O UR TEST HAS ASKED you to work in two cultural codes, as those who try it quickly realize. On the one hand, students have described their lives from a stance that reflects the diverse cultures and language of Bronx youth. Yet the questions that follow those passages take the well-known approach and voice of tests like the SAT. To answer, readers must switch to another code, familiar to standardized test takers, as they analyze texts that present the student experience.

We hope that taking the test will prove useful, as both youth and adults pay close attention to each code, figuring out what each passage and question set means. That very process may prompt important conversation and new learning, both separately and together. This section presents different ways to try it, suggested by those who took the test in its development stage.

→ Test-Taker Feedback

A student contributor drew this conclusion from schoolmates' response after taking the SAT Bronx.

DINAH | Our test would be a good way to introduce students to the SAT. They'll be taking a test that they're more comfortable with, and when they ultimately take the SAT, they'll feel more comfortable with it. Last year, two of my teachers gave their eleventh grade students a test from our book. I was walking down the hallway, and the eleventh graders were coming from class, and everybody was so excited: "Did you just take that test? Did you see the things that were on it?" Everybody felt so encouraged and inspired. For once, they actually felt intelligent. They knew the answers, because they can relate to what we understand in our community.

FOR REFERENCE

▶ One of the surest predictors of how students will perform on the SAT is their family's income. For every $10,000 of additional family income, the SAT score climbs an average of about 10 points, according to statistics from the College Board.

▶ When the PSAT is taken first in the 10th grade and then in 11th grade, the 11th grade scores improve (on average, 3.3 points in reading, 4.4 in math and 4.1 in writing), according to the College Board. It is unclear, however, whether the boost comes because students are more familiar with the test or because they have an additional year of schooling.

▶ The $2-billion-a-year testing industry has little oversight from public agencies, and some critics are calling for the Federal government to take notice. Major scoring errors on the SAT tests given in October 2006 caused a furor, and an increase in state testing has made quality control in the industry even more difficult.

▶ High school grades are a better predictor of college success than are scores on the SAT. Over 760 accredited four-year colleges do not require either the SAT or its rival ACT test.

SUGGESTIONS FOR USE

FOR YOUTH

> Use *SAT Bronx* sections as practice for taking the actual College Board exams. It can help you get used to the ways testmakers include incorrect answers in the multiple choices —answers that may seem right at first glance, but are not supported by the passage.

> Make a list of subjects about which you know a lot, whether or not they are taught in school. Either by yourself or with a few other students, write a short passage about one such subject, along with several "test questions" based on that passage. Give your test to a few adults, and then talk with them about how they scored on it, and why.

> With other students, discuss some things you have in common with the Bronx students represented in this book, and some things you do not. On what basis might you try to assess someone's "intelligence" if you do not share a common experience?

FOR ADULTS

> Take a section of *SAT Bronx* with a group of other adults. What was difficult for you, if anything, about its passages or its questions? What might adults learn from that about the challenges students encounter in College Board–type tests?

> Use *SAT Bronx* sections as an entry point for talking about equity in the ways we assess readiness for college. What student strengths, if any, might tests like the PSAT and the SAT overlook? What actions could educators take to right such an imbalance?

THE STUDENT CONTRIBUTORS

Debbie Brown

Marcus Caceres

Erick Core

Adeyefa Finch

Karima Fyfield

Genesis Garcia

Markedia Hinds

Dinah Joshua

Josefina Medina

Crystal Parker

Donivan Spear

Sean Taylor

Travis Toledo

NOTE: Other than the names of these student
contributors, all names used in *SAT Bronx*
are fictional and bear no relation to any real
person, now or in the past.

ACKNOWLEDGMENTS

SAT Bronx began as the idea of Shannon O'Grady, an English teacher at Bronx Leadership Academy 2, who saw in her students more intelligence and promise than their SAT scores revealed. Encouraged by What Kids Can Do, she and her colleague, history teacher Kristin Ferrales, drew together a group of students to explore that observation, in a club that met twice weekly. We owe thanks to Paulette Franklin and Elyse Doti, administrators at BLA 2, for inviting WKCD's Kathleen Cushman into the school to work with that group throughout the year.

As Adobe Youth Voices launched its worldwide initiative with the goal of inspiring youth to "create with purpose," it recognized in *SAT Bronx* an opportunity to support another kind of learning. Student contributors to the project had the chance to learn book design and layout, moving their recorded voices to the printed page. In summer 2007, they gathered in ones and twos to try their hand at Creative Suite 2 software, which includes the publishing program InDesign. By making that exploration possible, Adobe opened new doors to these students, giving them skills that will last long after high school.

The students' volunteer design mentor was Kathryn Van Syckle, a young graphic artist and writer working at New York Magazine. This book's design grew from her generous tending over months and weekends and evenings. Often at her side, contributing astute editorial as well as design comments, were Bronx students Dinah Joshua, Markedia Hinds, Genesis Garcia, and Karima Fyfield. As the book developed, critical guidance also came from Eliza Miller, an editor with considerable recent test experience herself, and from WKCD's Abe Louise Young and Barbara Cervone. Sandra Delany made key adjustments to the final layout.

Chicago teacher, photographer, and writer Will Okun deserves warm thanks or contributing the cover photograph. Found among the many vivid images of youth on his website www.wjzo.com, it reminds us that powerful knowledge and experience live in all our urban youth, not just those in our own neighborhoods.